Introduction

The activities in this book have been carefully selected to give children a 'hands-on' introduction to science. In doing these simple experiments, children can make a variety of discoveries that will surprise and delight them. Above all, it is hoped that these activities will encourage children to explore and experiment further, because it is most valuable to discover for yourself the many possible outcomes science holds.

There are no 'wrong' outcomes to the activities – every finding is valid, and bound to stimulate lots of questions. The notes at the end of the book suggest explanations and insights into those science concepts that can be discussed simply with young children; questions about more complex concepts are better explored through 'hands-on' experimentation than by explanations too abstract for the very young. These notes also include the answers to special challenges scattered throughout the book.

The activities in this book have been tested and are safe when conducted as instructed. The publisher accepts no responsibility for any damage caused or sustained due to the use or misuse of ideas or materials featured in this book.

Egg Games

Did you know you can remove the shell of an egg without cracking it?

HERE'S HOW:

1. Carefully place an uncooked egg into a glass.

2. Add enough vinegar to cover the egg.

3. Wait for a day. Then gently lift the egg out of the glass. What does it feel like? What happens if you leave the egg covered in the vinegar for three or four days?

Have you ever tried to bounce an egg? Be sure to follow these steps before you do!

1. Place a hard-boiled egg in a glass.

2. Add enough vinegar to cover the egg.

3. After two days, how does the egg feel? Return the egg to the vinegar and wait one more day. Then gently bounce the egg. Try this in the kitchen sink first. How high can you bounce the egg?

That's really egg-citing!

HERE'S AN EGGS-TRA TRICK TO TRY: MAKE AN EGG FLOAT!

Place an uncooked egg in a glass of warm water and gently stir in a few spoonfuls of salt. Watch the egg rise.

Science Surprises

Gordon Penrose

Edited by
Janis Nostbakken

and
Marilyn Baillie

HODDER AND STOUGHTON
LONDON SYDNEY AUCKLAND TORONTO

Contents

Elec-tricks

Your hair will stand on end when you try this trick! It works best on a dry day and with squeaky clean hair.

HERE'S HOW:

1 Rub a blown-up balloon back and forth on your hair.

2 Look into a mirror and slowly pull the balloon away from your head.

3 Watch your hair rise!

4 Now hold the balloon against a wall. When you let it go, does it stick to the wall?

Can a comb pick up paper? Yes! . . . if it's full of static electricity.

1 Run a plastic comb through your hair several times.

2 Hold the comb near small pieces of tissue paper or bits of paper towel.

3 Watch the paper jump!

Watch the water wiggle!

YOU CAN MAKE WATER WIGGLE WITHOUT EVEN TOUCHING IT.

Turn on a cold water tap and let the water flow in a slow, steady stream. Then run a plastic comb through your hair. Hold the comb beside the stream of water. What happens to the water when you move the comb back and forth?

Presto! Change-o!

Make dull pennies dazzle!

HERE'S HOW:

1. Fill a glass half full of vinegar.
2. Drop in old, tarnished pennies and stir.
3. Spoon out the shiny coins. How long do they stay bright?

TRY THE SAME EXPERIMENT AGAIN, BUT WITH A TWIST.

This time add a pinch or two of salt to the vinegar. Does the same thing happen? Then add a heaped spoonful of salt to the vinegar. What happens when these coins are left out to dry?

What a BRIGHT idea!

Secret Messages

Send secret messages to a special friend!

HERE'S HOW:

1 Dip a toothpick or cotton swab in lemon juice and draw or print your message on plain paper.

2 Pour salt on the paper to completely cover the message.

3 When the paper is totally dry, brush away the salt.

4 To see the message, rub a pencil or crayon back and forth across the paper several times.

IF YOU WANT TO READ THIS SECRET MESSAGE, HOLD IT UP TO A MIRROR.

You can use mirror writing to send a secret message of your own. Simply write from right to left across the page, printing the letters of each word backwards.

11

Body Tricks

Surprise yourself with these body tricks.

HERE'S HOW:

Hop Stopper

1. Bend over and grab your toes.
2. Keep your knees slightly bent.
3. Try to hop forwards. Can you hop backwards?

Balancing Act

1. Balance on one foot and count to ten.
2. Have a rest.
3. Balance on one foot again, this time with your eyes closed. What number can you count to before you fall over?

QUICK! WHICH IS BIGGER, YOUR FOOT OR YOUR FOREARM?

Find out for sure by measuring your foot from heel to toe with a ruler or measuring tape. Then measure your arm from wrist to elbow. Were you right?

Taste Test

Which would you rather eat, a raw potato or a raw apple? Take a taste test to find out.

HERE'S HOW:

1. Start with peeled slices of uncooked potato and apple.

2. Cover your eyes with a blindfold.

3. Tightly hold your nose with one hand.

4. Take a bite of each slice.
   Can you tell which is which?

TRY THE SAME TEST WITH FRUIT JUICE.

Hold your nose and take a sip of grape juice, then of apple juice. Can you tell them apart?

The nose knows!

Eye Openers

**Can you really believe what you see?
Look carefully at each of these
pictures to find out.**

1 How many faces do you see?

2 Which flower centre
is the smallest?

3 How many animals can you find here?

4 Stare at the black squares and count to ten. What else do you see?

5 Are these stars the same colour?

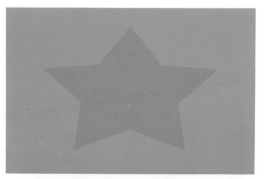

Answers on page 31

Wow! A floating finger!

MAKE YOUR OWN OPTICAL ILLUSION.

Hold your index fingers slightly apart in front of your eyes. Stare at an object beyond your fingers. What do you see floating between your fingers?

Fingerprints

**True or false? All members of
your family have the same fingerprints.
Find the answer by collecting and
comparing the fingerprints of your
family and friends. Be sure to wash
your hands before and after
following these steps.**

1. Lightly rub a thin coating of lipstick on to your fingertip.

2. Carefully place your smudged finger on a piece of clear sticky tape.

3. Peel the tape off your finger and stick it on to a piece of clean paper.

WHICH FINGERPRINT TYPE IS THE MOST COMMON?

Once you've collected prints of
a number of people, compare
them to each other and to
these fingerprint types.

Are you
a loop,
a whorl or
an arch?

Arch

Loop

Whorl

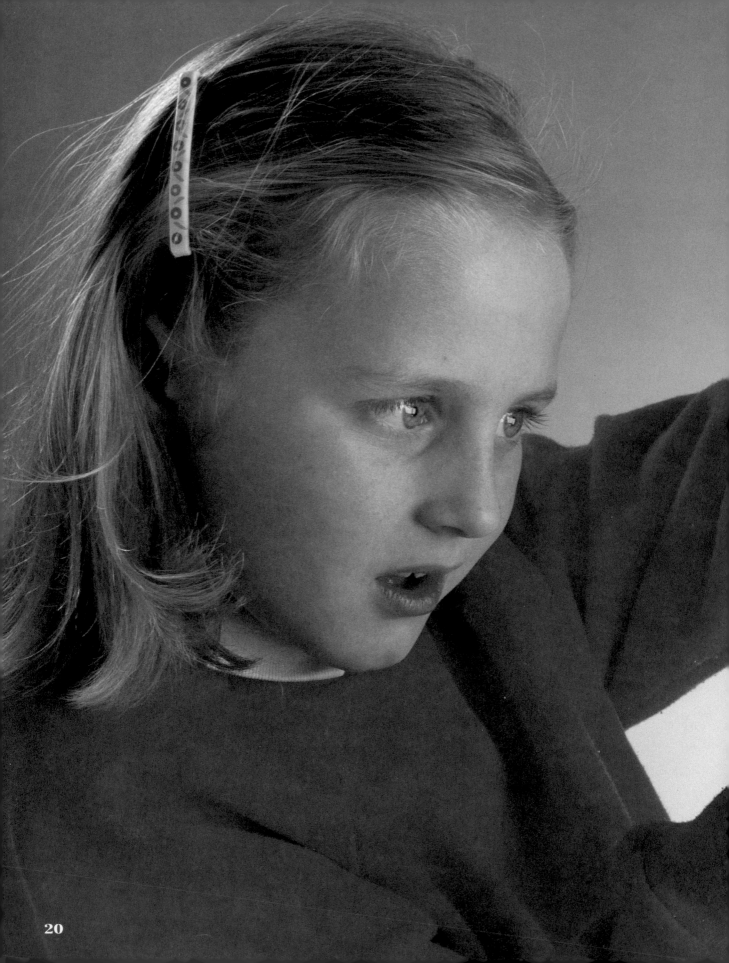

Lost and Found

Make a coin disappear right before your very eyes!

HERE'S HOW:

1 Fill a glass with water.

2 Put a coin in the palm of your hand.

3 Place the glass on top of the coin and look down through it to see the coin.

4 Now put your other hand on top of the glass and look for the coin through the side of the glass. Is it still there?

TRY THIS PENCIL TRICK!

Stick a pencil in a glass of water and look at it through the side of the glass. What happens to the pencil?

How did it break?

Finger Power

Pick a partner (even one bigger than yourself!) and prove how much power you have in your fingers.

HERE'S HOW:

The Mighty Finger

1 Ask your partner to sit in a straight-backed chair with arms folded, chin up, head high.

2 Press your index finger against your partner's forehead. Can your partner get up out of the chair?

Fighting Fingers

1 Ask your partner to stand with arms fully outstretched and fists pressed firmly together, one on top of the other.

2 Hold out your index fingers and quickly strike them sideways, in opposite directions, against the fists. Can your partner still hold the fists together?

Be a penny pincher!

NOW TEST YOUR FINGER POWER AGAINST A PENNY.

Put your knuckles together. Ask your partner to help you raise your ring fingers and place a penny between them. Here's the challenge: can you drop the penny?

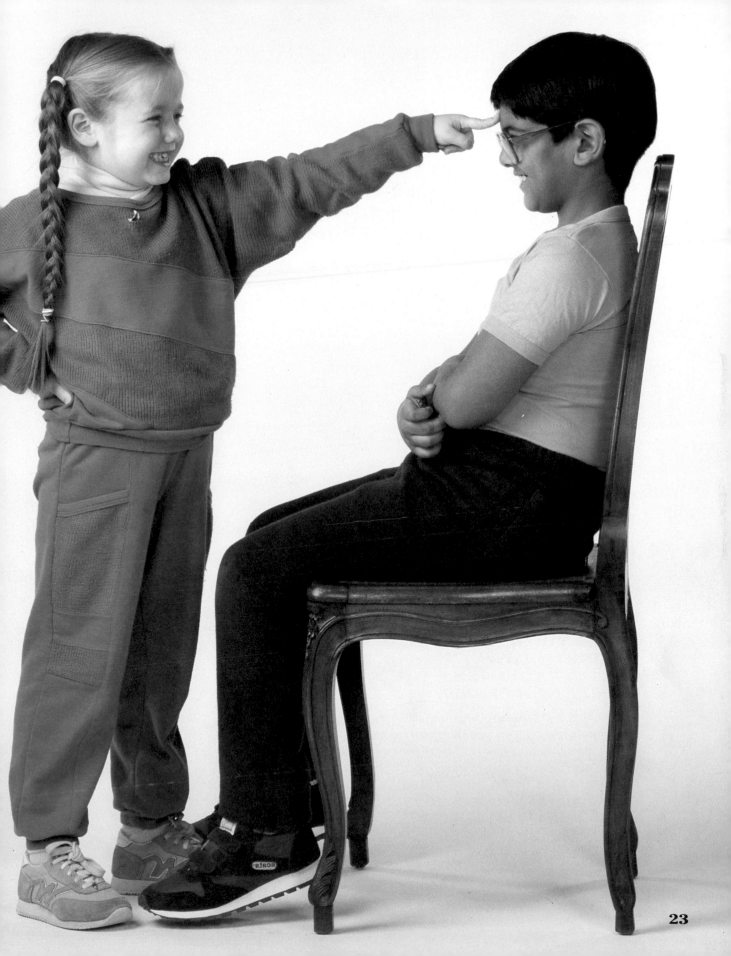

Hole in Your Hand

**Do you have X-ray vision?
Follow these steps to see a hole
right through your hand!**

1 Roll a piece of paper about 30 cm long into a tube or use an empty paper towel roll.

2 Look straight ahead at some object or spot on the wall.

3 Hold the tube up to one eye so that it completely covers the eye.

4 Hold your other hand, palm open and facing you, half-way along the tube.

5 Keep looking at the object with both eyes.

   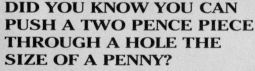

DID YOU KNOW YOU CAN PUSH A TWO PENCE PIECE THROUGH A HOLE THE SIZE OF A PENNY?

Cut a penny-sized hole in the centre of a piece of paper. Fold the paper in half. Then place the coin in the centre of the fold. Hold the outer edges of the fold, pull upwards and wiggle the paper back and forth to ease the two pence piece through the hole.

The penny's dropped!

High and Dry

What goes under water but never gets wet? Follow these steps to find the answer.

1 Fill a sink or basin with water.

2 Pack some tissue into the bottom of a drinking glass so that it stays in place when the glass is turned upside down.

3 Hold the glass upside down and push it straight into the water without tipping it.

4 Pull the glass straight up out of the water. Now pull out the tissue. Is it wet or dry? What happens when you tip the glass?

HOW MANY TIMES CAN YOU FOLD A PIECE OF PAPER IN HALF? TWENTY, THIRTY, FORTY TIMES?

Guess again and then try folding paper yourself to see if you are right. Use any kind of paper, from tissue to cardboard.

27

Card Trick

**With a flick of your finger
you can drop a coin into a glass
without touching it.**

HERE'S HOW:

1 Place a playing card on top of a glass.

2 Put a coin on top of the card.

3 Quickly flick your index finger against the edge of the card. The card flies off, but what happens to the coin?

**YOU CAN DROP A PENNY INTO
A SQUASH BOTTLE TOO.**

Balance the coin on top of a strip of paper placed on top of an open bottle. Quickly pull the strip of paper out from under the penny.

What a way to save money!

There's SCIENCE everywhere!

Notes

Egg Games
(page 4)
Activity No. 1

Eggshells contain calcium; so do your bones and teeth. It helps make them strong. Vinegar is an acid which dissolves the calcium in the shell leaving the skin under the shell to hold the egg together. In much the same way as the vinegar, acids in your mouth attack your teeth and make holes in them. That's why brushing your teeth is so important.

Activity No. 3

At first the egg sinks, because it is heavier than water. But when you add salt, the water becomes heavier than the egg, and so the egg floats. This is why it is easier for you to float in salt water than in fresh water.

Elec-tricks
(page 6)
Activities Nos. 1, 2 and 3

The balloon and comb pick up static electricity from your hair. Have you ever felt static electricity when you shuffle across a carpet in stockinged feet?

Presto! Change-o!
(page 8)
Activities Nos. 1 and 2

In time, pennies become dirty. Vinegar is an acid that eats away the dirt to leave the pennies clean and shiny. Salt combines with the vinegar to form a stronger acid that works even faster. When the pennies cleaned with salt and vinegar are left out in the air, they turn green. If you don't want your pennies to turn green, wash them with detergent as soon as you take them out of the salt and vinegar mixture, then rinse and dry them.

Secret Messages
(page 11)
Activity No. 1

When you brush away the salt, you leave a trail of small salt crystals with sharp edges on your message. As you rub the pencil over the paper, more lead catches on the salt crystals than on the rest of the paper. That's why your secret message appears.

Activity No. 2

You can read the secret message in the mirror because it is written backwards. The mirror flips the printing in the same way that it flips your image when you look in the mirror.

Body Tricks
(page 12)
Activity No. 2

Eyesight is one of the senses that affects your balance. Standing on one leg unbalances you. Take away your sight, too, and your body cannot stay upright.

Activity No. 3

Your foot and forearm are exactly the same size! This is true for people of all ages.

Taste Test
(page 15)
Activities Nos. 1 and 2

Your tongue can only tell you if food is sweet, sour, salty or bitter. You need your sense of smell to tell one food's flavour from another.

Eye Openers
(pages 16-17)
Activities Nos. 1 and 2

Optical illusions can trick your eyes and fool your brain.

Answers to
Activity No. 1

1. There are four faces.
2. All of the flower centres are the same size.
3. There are two animals: a rabbit and a duck.
4. Grey dots appear and disappear.
5. Yes, both stars are the same colour.

Fingerprints
(page 18)
Activity No. 1

No two people in the world have the same fingerprints, not even identical twins. Did you know that no two cats have the same nose prints?

Activity No. 2

Loops are the most common fingerprint type.

Lost and Found
(page 21)
Activities Nos. 1 and 2

Even though water is clear, looking through it changes the way you see things. When you look through the water at an angle, you cannot see the coin. Pour the water out and look through the glass at the same angle. Now you can see the coin. In much the same way, when you look through the water at an angle, the pencil appears to be broken, but it you pour the water out, it looks whole again.

Finger Power
(page 22)
Activity No. 1

When sitting, all your partner's weight is in his or her seat. To stand up, your partner's head must move forward. Your finger stops the head from moving, the weight from shifting and your partner from standing.

Activity No. 2

Fingers win over fists every time. Your partner is pressing the fists together in an up-and-down direction. Your fingers attack on the sides where the fists are the weakest.

Activity No. 3

You cannot drop the penny. If your middle finger cannot move, neither can your ring finger, because the tendons of these fingers are joined together.

Hole in Your Hand (page 24)
Activity No. 1

You use both your eyes to see an object. Your brain receives a message from each eye and combines them to make the total picture. But in this trick, one eye sees your hand and the other sees the opening through the tube. When these two pictures are combined, you think you see a hole in your hand.

High and Dry (page 26)
Activity No. 1

Air gets trapped inside the glass and pushes against the water. The air keeps the water out of the glass and the paper stays dry.

Activity No. 2

It is impossible to fold any piece of paper in half more than nine times.

Card Trick (page 29)
Activities Nos. 1 and 2

When you flick the card, it moves so quickly that it flies right out from under the coin. The coin drops into the glass. In much the same way, the penny drops into the squash bottle when you quickly pull the strip of paper away.

British Library Cataloguing in Publication Data

Penrose, Gordon, *1925–*
Science surprises.
1. Science
I. Title   II. Nostbakken, Janis   III. Baillie, Marilyn
500

ISBN 0-340-55379-0 (hbk)
ISBN 0-340-54906-8 (pbk)

First published 1989 by Greey de Pencier Books, Toronto, Canada
First published in Great Britain 1991

Published by Hodder and Stoughton Children's Books,
a division of Hodder and Stoughton Ltd,
Mill Road, Dunton Green, Sevenoaks, Kent TN13 2YA

Photography: Ray Boudreau and Tony Thomas (page 13)
Illustrations: Tina Holdcroft and Andrew Plewes (pages 16-17)

Printed in Hong Kong